PRE-ALGEBRA

by
Sharon Vogt

Illustrated by
David Van Etten

Cover Design by
Peggy Jackson

Published by Instructional Fair • TS Denison
an imprint of

McGraw-Hill
Children's Publishing

About the Author

Sharon Vogt received her bachelor's degree in math education at Northeast Missouri State University. After graduating she spent several years teaching math to students in grades five through eight in a parochial school in St. Charles, Missouri. She received her master's degree from Webster University in 1991. Sharon then worked for a local publishing house and later became involved in editing workbook pages for a major textbook publisher. This is where Ms. Vogt found her true calling. Since then, she has been creating and editing math educational materials.

Recently Sharon fulfilled one of her life-long dreams and moved to Massachusetts where she can bask in the snow and learn first hand about her mother's heritage. She lives in the more rural, western side of the state with her dog, Tinker, and her cat, Fish. She is the producer of a math contest on America Online and the manager of a message area for math teachers.

McGraw-Hill
Children's Publishing

A Division of The **McGraw·Hill** Companies

Published by Instructional Fair • TS Denison
An imprint of McGraw-Hill Children's Publishing
Copyright © 1996 McGraw-Hill Children's Publishing

Send all inquiries to:
McGraw-Hill Children's Publishing
3195 Wilson Drive NW
Grand Rapids, Michigan 49544

Pre-Algebra
ISBN: 1-56822-342-0

Table of Contents

Fractions, Decimals, and Percents

Adding and Subtracting Fractions . . 1
Multiplying Fractions 2
Dividing Fractions 3
Working with Mixed Numbers 4
Problem Solving with Fractions 5
Adding and Subtracting Decimals . . 6
Multiplying and Dividing Decimals . 7
Working with Percents 9
Problem Solving with Decimals . . . 10
Mixed Review 11

Integers and Rational Numbers

What are Integers 12
Adding Integers 13
Subtracting Integers 14
Multiplying and Dividing Integers . 15
Mixed Review 16
Order of Operations 17
Rational Numbers 18
Comparing Rational Numbers . . . 19
Mixed Review 20

Variables

Letter Soup 21
Simplifying Expressions 23
Number Lines 24
Variables and Number Lines 25
Mixed Review 27
Number Statements 28
Algebraic Expressions 29
Writing Algebraic Expressions . . . 30

Equations and Inequalities

Solving Equations 31
Mixed Practice Solving Equations . 33
Problem Solving with Equations . . . 34
Solving Multi-Step Equations 35
Solving Equations 37
Mixed Review 38
Problem Solving 39
Solving Inequalities 41
Mixed Practice 43

Graphing

Plotting Points 44
Graphing Equations 46
Solving for y 48
Slope 49
Finding Equations 51
Graphing Using the Short-Cut
  Method 52
Mixed Review
  Equations and Inequalities 54

Answer Key 57

About This Book

Algebra is a branch of mathematics that we use a great deal, but often do not realize that we are using it. Children begin using algebra in the first or second grade. Algebra, in short, is a mathematical way of finding missing information. It is the basis for most other higher math courses.

The extra practice activities in this book cover the basics of pre-algebra while reviewing other topic associated with basic math. The examples provided include step-by-step instructions. Activities are appropriate for those who need a little extra help when learning about algebra for the first time and also serve as excellent resources for those who need a review of basic mathematics and algebra skills before taking a more advanced algebra class.

Use this book to suit your own needs. Choose those topics that focus on the help you need. Read over the directions and then work through the activities. Check your answers by referring to the answer key.

A mixed review is provided at several points throughout the book. Each review covers most of the important skills that are covered from the beginning of the book. Completing these exercises will let you know how well you remember what you have learned. If you have forgotten how to solve a problem, refer to the section on that topic and review again. By reviewing those skills where you may be experiencing problems, you will better understand those skills and gain the confidence needed to work similar problems in the future.

Adding and Subtracting Fractions

When you add or subtract fractions, you always have to have fractions with *common denominators*. (The denominator is the the number below the fraction bar.) To find a denominator both fractions can share, find the denominators' least common multiple.

Find the least common denominator (or least common multiple) for each pair of fractions.

1. $\frac{2}{3}$ and $\frac{3}{4}$ 2. $\frac{1}{9}$ and $\frac{1}{3}$ 3. $\frac{5}{6}$ and $\frac{4}{9}$

Multiples

3	4
3	4
6	8
9	12
12	16

_____ 12 _____   _____   _____

Add or subtract. Reduce to lowest terms.

4. $\frac{1}{2}$ 5. $\frac{2}{7}$ 6. $\frac{3}{5}$

   $+\frac{2}{5}$ $+\frac{3}{4}$ $+\frac{7}{10}$

7. $\frac{4}{9}$ 8. $\frac{7}{10}$ 9. $\frac{2}{3}$

   $-\frac{1}{6}$ $-\frac{1}{6}$ $-\frac{2}{9}$

10. Terry is building a bookshelf. She needs one long board she can cut into two pieces. She needs one piece ¾ yd. long and another piece ⅛ yd. long. What length board does she need? _____

Multiplying Fractions

Canceling is a "short-cut" method to multiplying fractions. Anytime the numerator (top number) and the denominator (bottom number) are both divisible by the same number, you can take a short-cut.

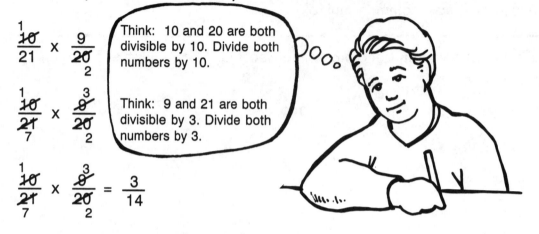

Think: 10 and 20 are both divisible by 10. Divide both numbers by 10.

Think: 9 and 21 are both divisible by 3. Divide both numbers by 3.

Solve the following problems:

1. $\dfrac{2}{5} \times \dfrac{7}{8} =$

2. $\dfrac{4}{9} \times \dfrac{3}{8} =$

3. $\dfrac{11}{12} \times \dfrac{8}{11} =$

4. $\dfrac{9}{20} \times \dfrac{8}{9} =$

5. $\dfrac{6}{15} \times \dfrac{21}{36} =$

6. $\dfrac{25}{26} \times \dfrac{2}{15} =$

7. $\dfrac{9}{30} \times \dfrac{6}{27} =$

8. $\dfrac{3}{11} \times \dfrac{8}{12} =$

9. $\dfrac{14}{45} \times \dfrac{15}{21} =$

10. $\dfrac{4}{25} \times \dfrac{20}{22} =$

11. $\dfrac{2}{3} \times \dfrac{9}{13} =$

12. $\dfrac{27}{38} \times \dfrac{26}{45} =$

13. $\dfrac{44}{57} \times \dfrac{1}{4} \times \dfrac{49}{55} =$

14. $\dfrac{6}{7} \times \dfrac{28}{30} \times \dfrac{17}{32} =$

Dividing Fractions

Multiplying and dividing fractions are almost the same. You have to remember only one more step when dividing fractions. Always flip the second number, the number you are dividing by. This changes the division problem to a multiplication problem.

$$\frac{6}{7} \div \frac{15}{21}$$

$$\frac{\cancel{6}^{2}}{\cancel{7}_{1}} \times \frac{\cancel{21}^{3}}{\cancel{15}_{5}} = \frac{6}{5} = 1\frac{1}{5}$$

Flip
Cancel
Multiply

1. Theo, Tyrone, and Terese sold candy bars to earn some extra money. They decided to divide their earnings evenly. Altogether they earned $24. Describe how you can use division to determine how much money each person earned.

_____

2. Describe another method to solve the same problem. This time use a fraction and multiplication.

_____

Solve the following problems:

3. $\frac{2}{3} \div \frac{7}{12} =$ 4. $\frac{4}{7} \div \frac{12}{17} =$ 5. $\frac{10}{21} \div \frac{5}{14} =$

6. $\frac{6}{7} \div \frac{2}{35} =$ 7. $\frac{11}{32} \div \frac{7}{24} =$ 8. $\frac{1}{2} \div \frac{5}{7} =$

9. $\frac{18}{56} \div \frac{27}{32} =$ 10. $\frac{15}{42} \div \frac{25}{36} =$ 11. $\frac{32}{51} \div \frac{17}{21} =$

Working with Mixed Numbers

Subtraction:

$$6\frac{1}{4} = 6\frac{3}{12} = \cancel{6}\,\overset{5}{\cancel{6}}\,\overset{15}{\cancel{\frac{3}{12}}}$$

$$-2\frac{2}{3} = 2\frac{8}{12} = 2\frac{8}{12}$$

$$\overline{3\frac{7}{12}}$$

Think: When subtracting the fractional part, I can't subtract 8 from 3. I must borrow from the 6. One whole is the same as $\frac{12}{12}$.

Multiplication:

$$4\frac{1}{2} \times 5 = \frac{9}{2} \times \frac{5}{1} = \frac{45}{2} = 22\frac{1}{2}$$

Solve the following problems:

1. $\begin{array}{r} 3\frac{1}{2} \\ + 5\frac{1}{3} \\ \hline \end{array}$

2. $\begin{array}{r} 5\frac{5}{6} \\ - 2\frac{1}{8} \\ \hline \end{array}$

3. $\begin{array}{r} 12\frac{2}{3} \\ + 7\frac{3}{5} \\ \hline \end{array}$

4. $\begin{array}{r} 19\frac{2}{9} \\ - 9\frac{2}{3} \\ \hline \end{array}$

5. $\begin{array}{r} 40\frac{11}{12} \\ + 22\frac{3}{4} \\ \hline \end{array}$

6. $\begin{array}{r} 26\frac{14}{25} \\ - 21\frac{3}{5} \\ \hline \end{array}$

7. $4\frac{2}{7} \times 6\frac{1}{5} =$

8. $3\frac{5}{6} \times 4\frac{1}{2} =$

9. $10\frac{2}{7} \times 14 =$

10. $24 \div 6\frac{3}{4} =$

11. $6\frac{1}{8} \div 2\frac{1}{12} =$

12. $12\frac{5}{9} \div 6\frac{1}{3} =$

Problem Solving with Fractions

Use what you know about fractions and mixed numbers to solve the following problems.

1. Kenneth is planning to build a wooden fence to surround a rectangular portion of his yard. He will use the house to block off one side. The house is 18⅓ yds long. He wants the width of the fenced area to be 10 yds. What is the perimeter of this area? _____

2. What is the area of Kenneth's yard? (Hint: To find the area of a rectangle, multiply the length by the width.) _____

3. Kenneth purchased wood beams that are 5 yds long. He will use the beams to make posts that are 1⅙ yds long. How many posts can he cut from each beam? _____

4. How much wood will be left over from each beam?

_____

5. Kenneth is going to put one post every 5 feet. A post will be at every corner, including the corners made by the house and the fence. How many posts will Kenneth need? (Hint: Draw a picture to help see this problem more clearly.) _____

Adding and Subtracting Decimals

Decimals are added and subtracted in the same way as whole numbers. There are two simple rules to keep in mind.

1. Always keep the decimal points lined up.
   4.7 + 15 + 112.03 can also be written as

$$\begin{array}{r} 4.7 \\ 15 \\ \underline{112.03} \end{array}$$

2. When subtracting, you must always have a number to subtract from. If the space is empty, fill it in with a zero. To solve 15.7 – 10.26, put a zero after the seven. When you subtract 6, you can borrow.

NO	Yes
15.7	15.70
$\underline{-10.26}$	$\underline{-10.26}$
5.56	5.44

Solve the following problems:

1. $\begin{array}{r} 4.7 \\ 61.45 \\ \underline{+\ 7.09} \end{array}$

2. $\begin{array}{r} 6.09 \\ 19.1 \\ \underline{+\ 16.11} \end{array}$

3. $\begin{array}{r} 14 \\ 41.51 \\ \underline{+\ 119.8} \end{array}$

4. $\begin{array}{r} 57.23 \\ \underline{-\ 14.3} \end{array}$

5. $\begin{array}{r} 19.7 \\ \underline{-\ 7.18} \end{array}$

6. $\begin{array}{r} 81 \\ \underline{-\ 5.23} \end{array}$

7. 47.5 + 16.98

8. 121.7 – 98.26

9. 41.56 – 27.9

_____   _____   _____

10. Dr. Weinhaus is conducting an experiment. An object weighs 4 mg before the experiment and 2.59 mg afterwards. How much weight does the object lose? _____

11. In a second experiment, the same object loses 1.78 mg. What is the weight of the object after the experiment? _____

Multiplying and Dividing Decimals

1. Multiply as if you were multiplying whole numbers.
2. Add the number of digits after the decimal point for each number being multiplied.
3. Place the decimal point so that the answer has the number of digits after the decimal point found in step 2.

```
  25.6     1 decimal place
x 1.32     2 decimal places
  512      3 decimal places
 7680
25600
33.792
```

1. Move the decimal in the divisor to make a whole number.
2. Move the same number of places in the dividend and carry the decimal point up to the line.
3. Divide as usual.

```
        0.455
3.2 | 1.4560
      128
      176
      160
      160
      160
        0
```

Solve the following problems:

1.
```
   2.04
 x 5.8
```

2.
```
   61.9
 x 0.03
```

3.
```
   0.14
 x 0.7
```

4.
```
   9.007
 x 8.12
```

5.
```
   81.25
 x 12.6
```

6. 6.4 | 0.256

7. 0.15 | 0.471

8. 2.9 | 226.2

9. 19.1 | 108.87

Percents

Fractions, decimals, and percents are all related. Equivalent amounts can be written in all three forms.

The fraction bar is the same as a division sign.

$\frac{5}{8} = 5 \div 8 = 0.625$

Decimals can be written as fractions by recalling a decimal's name.
0.625 is read, "625 thousandths"

$\frac{625}{1000}$ is read, "625 thousandths"

$0.625 = \frac{625}{1000} = \frac{5}{8}$

To change a decimal to a percent, move the decimal point 2 places to the right. To change a percent to a decimal, move the decimal point 2 places to the left.

$0.625 = 62.5\%$

Complete the chart.

	Fraction	Decimal	Percent
1.	$\frac{2}{5}$		
2.	$\frac{3}{4}$		
3.		.25	
4.		0.675	
5.			50%
6.			87.5%
7.	$6\frac{7}{10}$		
8.		4.8	
9.			625%

Working with Percents

The word *percent* means "parts of a hundred." When you are working with percents, you are finding parts of a hundred. Fifty percent is the same as 50:100 or *fifty out of every hundred*. If a weather forecaster said that 50% of the year the days would be sunny, you would know that 50 out of every 100 days in the year would be sunny. To find out exactly how many days that is, just multiply. But change the percent to a decimal first.

50% x 365 = 0.5 x 365 = 182.5

If the forecaster is correct, about 183 days should be sunny.

Solve the following problems:

1. 40% of 120 is _____.

2. 30% of 900 is _____.

3. 75% of $125 is _____.

4. 25% of $15.65 is _____.

5. 6.5% of 14 is _____.

6. 610% of 42 is _____.

7. Jane is buying a bicycle that is on sale for 35% off the original price. Before the sale, the price was $212. How much will Jane have to pay for the bike? _____

8. Sam read a sales ad for his favorite music store. It is having a 40% off sale. CDs regularly cost $21 and cassettes, $15. What is the sale price for these items? _____

9. Julio has $25 to spend on a pair of jeans. One style that normally sells for $35 is on sale at 35% off the original price. Does he have enough money to buy the jeans? _____

Problem Solving with Decimals

1. Karyn is buying a CD for her friend's birthday present. She has only $25 to spend. If tax is 5.25%, will she have enough money to buy the CD?

_____

2. Describe one way you could solve problem #1 without doing any calculations. Can you use logic instead? _____

_____

_____

3. The T-shirts have been discounted twice. Are the two discounts equal to one 55% discount? Find the cost of one T-shirt with a 55% discount. Then find the cost taking the two discounts separately.

_____

4. Tomas was given a $50 gift certificate for his birthday. He wants to buy two T-shirts and three cassettes. Will the certificate pay for everything? How much will the total purchase cost?

_____

Mixed Review

Solve the following problems

1. $2\frac{1}{3}$
   $+ 8\frac{5}{8}$

2. $6\frac{7}{8}$
   $- 1\frac{3}{10}$

3. $3\frac{1}{6} \times 18 =$

4. $5.1\overline{)23.97}$

5. $\quad 6.79$
   $\times 0.18$

6. $\quad 14.2$
   $\quad 196$
   $+ 8.01$

7. $2\frac{3}{4} \div \frac{3}{8} =$

8. $\frac{1}{7} \times 4\frac{3}{9} \times 2\frac{1}{3} =$

9. $\quad 47.9$
   $+ 16.015$

	Fraction	Decimal	Percent
10.	$\frac{1}{8}$		
11.		1.7	
12.			65%

Complete the chart.

13. Paul took four tests on Monday. He received an A on 50% of them and a B on 25% of them. On how many tests did Paul not receive an A or a B? _____

14. Mrs. Lombardo earned $370 from her job. She put 25% of this money into a savings account. How much money did she save?

_____

What Are Integers?

Integers are the opposites of counting numbers. They are found on the number line on the right side of zero. As you move to the left on the number line, the numbers get smaller.

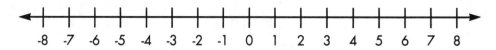

Absolute value is the value of a distance on the number line. The distance from -8 to -2 is 6. Even though the distance describes an area on the negative side of the number line, it is still positive.

$$| -6 | = 6$$
The absolute value of -6 is 6.

The absolute value of any positive or negative number is positive.

Fill in the blanks with <, >, or =.

1. -8 _____ 6

2. 10 _____ 4

3. 0 _____ -2

4. -9 _____ -7

5. 9 _____ -9

6. -1 _____ -2

7. |5| _____ 5

8. |-5| _____ -5

9. |-5| _____ 5

10. |-8| _____ 10

11. |9| _____ -2

12. |-3| _____ |-6|

13. The distance on the number line from 1 to 7 is _____ .

14. The distance on the number line from -1 to -7 is _____ .

15. The distance on the number line from 1 to -7 is _____ .

Adding Integers

$$\xleftarrow{\hspace{1em}} \overset{\displaystyle \text{-8 -7 -6 -5 -4 -3 -2 -1 0 1 2 3 4 5 6 7 8}}{\underset{}{\left|\;\right|\;\left|\;\right|\;\left|\;\right|\;\left|\;\right|\;\left|\;\right|}} \xrightarrow{\hspace{1em}}$$

+ tells you to move in the positive direction, or to the right.
- tells you to move in the negative direction, or to the left.
If two signs are together, **-** wins out over **+** .

$$-5 + 6 = 1 \qquad\qquad 4 + \text{-}6 = -2$$
$$6 + 4 = 10 \qquad\qquad -5 + \text{-}2 = -7$$

Solve the following problems:

1. $4 + \text{-}3 =$ 2. $8 + \text{-}4 =$ 3. $-2 + 10 =$

4. $-8 + 3 =$ 5. $4 + \text{-}7 =$ 6. $-2 + 4 =$

7. $3 + 8 =$ 8. $-3 + \text{-}8 =$ 9. $-4 + 4 =$

10. $5 + \text{-}5 =$ 11. $-6 + \text{-}2 =$ 12. $9 + 3 =$

13. $3 + \text{-}7 =$ 14. $-1 + 0 =$ 15. $-8 + 10 =$

16. $-19 + 7 =$ 17. $-14 + \text{-}22 =$ 18. $21 + \text{-}11 =$

19. Kenisha owes her mom $15. She gave her mom $7 to pay off part of what she owes. How much more does Kenisha owe?

    $-\$15 + \$7 = $ _____

Subtracting Integers

The same rules apply here as when adding integers, with only one exception.

$$\longleftarrow \!\!\!\!\!\!\!\! \begin{array}{cccccccccccccccccc} | & | & | & | & | & | & | & | & | & | & | & | & | & | & | & | & | \\ \text{-8} & \text{-7} & \text{-6} & \text{-5} & \text{-4} & \text{-3} & \text{-2} & \text{-1} & 0 & 1 & 2 & 3 & 4 & 5 & 6 & 7 & 8 \end{array} \!\!\!\!\!\!\!\! \longrightarrow$$

+ tells you to move in the positive direction, or to the right.

- tells you to move in the negative direction, or to the left.

If two signs are together, **-** wins out over **+** .

If two **-** signs are together, they cancel each other and become **+**.

$$9 - 10 = -1 \qquad\qquad -8 - -4 = -4$$
$$5 - -2 = 7 \qquad\qquad -6 - 3 = -9$$

Solve the following problems:

1. 6 – 5 =

2. 3 – 7 =

3. 2 – 6 =

4. -5 – -2 =

5. -8 – -8 =

6. -3 – -1 =

7. 4 – -9 =

8. 6 – -7 =

9. 3 – -3 =

10. -4 – -7 =

11. -6 – -2 =

12. -5 – -9 =

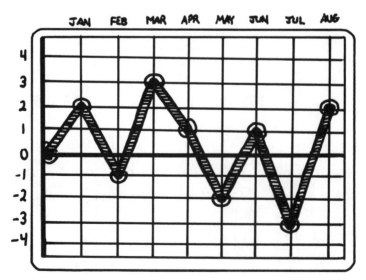

Multiplying and Dividing Integers

The rules for multiplying and dividing integers are few. They are easy to remember because they are similar to the rules for addition and subtraction.

+ x (or ÷) + = +

+ x (or ÷) - = -   - overpowers + .

- x (or ÷) - = +   Two -s make a + .

8 x 3 = 24   -6 x -5 = 30

-8 x 2 = -16   5 x -7 = -35

Solve the following problems:

1. 8 x -2

2. 6 x -1

3. 0 x -8

4. -6 x 7

5. -8 x 4

6. -7 x 8

7. -4 x -3

8. -6 x -6

9. -1 x -9

10. -15 ÷ 3

11. -16 ÷ -4

12. -24 ÷ +3

13. 20 ÷ -4

14. 81 ÷ -9

15. -18 ÷ -2

16. -26 x 12

17. 125 ÷ -5

18. -50 x -20

19. Matthew wrote six checks to pay bills. Every check was for the same amount, $24. How did his checking account balance change after writing the checks?

6 x -$24 = _____

Mixed Review

Solve the following problems:

1. $\frac{5}{8} \times 2\frac{4}{5} =$

2. $0.51\overline{)2.601}$

3.
$$\begin{array}{r} 3.127 \\ 17.5 \\ 81 \\ + \ 7.6 \end{array}$$

4.
$$\begin{array}{r} 8\frac{1}{8} \\ 2\frac{1}{6} \\ + \end{array}$$

5.
$$\begin{array}{r} 6\frac{2}{3} \\ 1\frac{8}{9} \\ - \end{array}$$

6.
$$\begin{array}{r} 6.71 \\ \times \ 2.6 \end{array}$$

7. 7% of 147 =

8. 512% of 26 =

9. 0.25% of 2,000 =

10. 25 + -6 =

11. -25 − 10 =

12. -19 − -30 =

13. -15 × 7 =

14. -84 ÷ -3 =

15. | -6 + -10 | =

Order of Operations

Please **E**xcuse **M**y **D**ear **A**unt **S**ally

P - Parentheses

E - Exponents

M - Multiplication and **D** - Division

A - Addition and **S** - Subtraction

Multiplication and division are equal operations. So are addition and subtraction. Equal operations can be calculated during the same step. Solve in the order you read from left to right.

Remember that parentheses, · , and x can all be used as notation for multiplication.

Solve the following problems:

1. $-5 + 2(8 - -6) - 4^2$

　$^-$P　$-5 + 2(14) - 4^2$

　E　$-5 + 2(14) - 16$

　M　$-5 + 28 - 16$

A/S　$23 - 16 = 7$

2. $15 + 6 \cdot -4 \div (-7 + 4)$

3. $40 \div (18 + -10) + 7^3$

4. $-52 + 5(-16 - -30) \div (-10 + 3)$

5. $24 \div |{-3} + 5| + -14 \cdot (-20 - -23) - 2^5$

Rational Numbers

Solve these problems, following the same rules you learned for integers.

1. $2\frac{3}{8} + -3\frac{1}{3} =$

2. $-16\frac{1}{9} - 7\frac{5}{6} =$

3. $\frac{2}{7} \times -4\frac{1}{5} =$

4. $-10\frac{2}{5} \div -5\frac{3}{10} =$

5. $12.47 + -8.2 =$

6. $127.6 + -63.15 + 2.9 =$

7. $-23.47 \times -8.7 =$

8. $-6.2\,\overline{)8.494}$

9. HiTech's stock sold for $31\frac{3}{8}$ on Monday. By Friday the same stock sold for $22\frac{1}{8}$. What was the change in the stock price?

_____

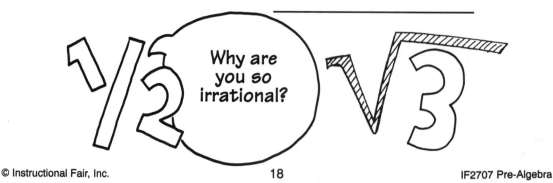

Why are you so irrational?

Comparing Rational Numbers

To compare fractions and decimals, first compare the whole number parts. If the whole number parts are the same, write amounts as all decimals or all fractions with common denominators.

$3\frac{1}{2}$? 3.27 -8.6 ? $-3\frac{2}{9}$

3.5 > 3.27 -8.6 < $-3\frac{2}{9}$

0.5 is larger than 0.27.   -8 is smaller than -3.

Fill each blank with <, >, or =.

1. 3.12 _____ $3\frac{3}{8}$

2. $5\frac{1}{4}$ _____ 5.7

3. $\frac{2}{3}$ _____ $\frac{3}{5}$

4. 9.7 _____ 9.75

5. $-\frac{4}{7}$ _____ $-\frac{1}{2}$

6. -5.6 _____ -5.72

7. 3.15 _____ $-6\frac{1}{8}$

8. $8\frac{4}{9}$ _____ -10.9

9. $\frac{3}{8}$ _____ 1.17

10. 8.15 _____ $3\frac{1}{5}$

Mixed Review

Solve the following problems:

1. $2\frac{7}{8} + -3\frac{1}{3} =$ 2. $5.12 + 2.6 =$ 3. $9\frac{1}{9} \times 6\frac{1}{6} =$

4. $4.9 \div 0.7 =$ 5. $6.2 \times -5.1 =$ 6. $-12 + -18 =$

7. $4.1 + 3.6 + -17.28 - 36.5 + 6.125 =$

8. $18 + 3 \cdot -6 \div |-7 -. 2| =$

9. $3^3 + -36 \div -9 + -16 =$

10. $62 + (17 + -21) \cdot 2^3 =$

Compare. Write <, >, or = in each blank.

11. -6 _____ $|-6|$

12. $3\frac{1}{4}$ _____ -4.18

13. 41.14 _____ $41\frac{1}{8}$

14. $12\frac{4}{9}$ _____ 12.5

                 IF2707 Pre-Algebra

Letter Soup

Variables are letters of the alphabet that step in for numbers. They are used in equations and formulas for changeable situations. The following is a formula to determine the cost of postage for making an item First Class. P stands for the amount of postage. The weight in ounces of the item is represented by w. To determine the cost of mailing a 3-oz. letter, replace the w with 3 and solve.

$$P = 0.32 + 0.23 (w - 1)$$
$$P (3 \text{ oz.}) = 0.32 + 0.23 (3 - 1)$$
$$P (3 \text{ oz.}) = 0.32 + 0.23 (2)$$
$$P (3 \text{ oz.}) = 0.32 + 0.46 = 0.78$$

You will need to put $0.78 postage on a letter that weighs 3 oz.

Replace the variables with the numbers shown and solve.

$$y = 3t + 15$$

1. $t = 7$

2. $t = 3.1$

$$x = 8.1s + t^2 - 11$$

3. $s = 37, t = 3$

4. $s = 0.4, t = 0.5$

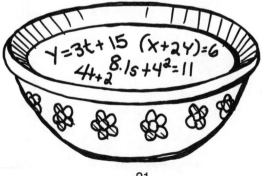

$$d = 3xz - z + 7y$$

5. $x = 1, y = 3, z = 2$ 6. $x = 5, y = 2, z = 12$

$$w = rst - (s + t^3)$$

7. $r = 2, s = 3, t = 6$ 8. $r = 6.5, s = 1, t = 0$

$$a = 11 - |17 - q^2|$$

9. $q = 6$ 10. $q = 4$

$$t = |g^3 - fgh| + fh$$

11. $f = 2.5, g = 2, h = 4$ 12. $f = 16, g = 1.1, h = 0$

Simplifying Expressions

Distributive Property

$$6(4x + 2) = (6 \cdot 4x) + (6 \cdot 2)$$
$$= 24x + 12$$

Combining Like Terms

$$3x + 6y - 2x + 7x = (3x - 2x + 7x) + 6y$$
$$= x(3 - 2 + 7) + 6y$$
$$= 8x + 6y$$

Simplify each expression.

1. $2(3x + 7) - 17$

2. $3.15 + 2y - 7.3 + 6y$

3. $5f + 2g - 6f$

4. $8(3xy + 2x) - 3z$

5. $14(5 - 3st) + 2st - 26$

6. $r(2s - 11) + 3r$

7. $\frac{1}{8}(x + 8y) - 2\frac{1}{4}x$

8. $4a + 3a - 17 + 8$

9. $16vw - 26vw + 8v - 6w$

10. $-7x - 2(-3x + 7) - 2x$

Number Lines

Number lines can be very helpful tools. Every real number has a place on the number line.

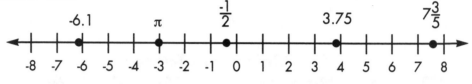

The numbers given below correspond to the points on the number line. Write the letter that names the point each number describes.

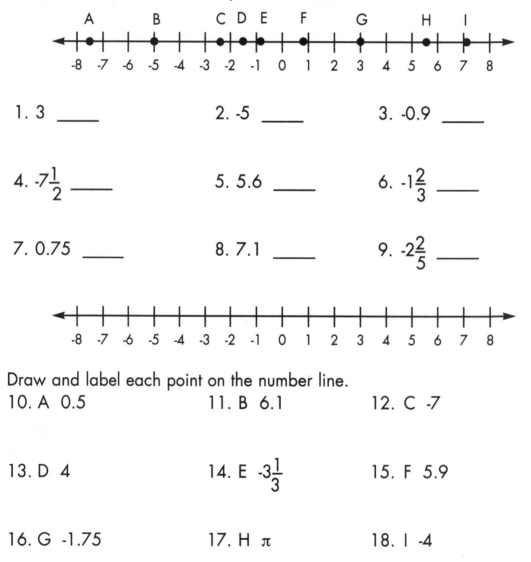

1. 3 _____

2. -5 _____

3. -0.9 _____

4. $-7\frac{1}{2}$ _____

5. 5.6 _____

6. $-1\frac{2}{3}$ _____

7. 0.75 _____

8. 7.1 _____

9. $-2\frac{2}{5}$ _____

Draw and label each point on the number line.

10. A 0.5

11. B 6.1

12. C -7

13. D 4

14. E $-3\frac{1}{3}$

15. F 5.9

16. G -1.75

17. H π

18. I -4

Variables and Number Lines

Variables are used to describe sets of numbers on a number line.

This set of numbers includes all numbers less than, but not equal to, 4. The circle on 4 is not filled in to show that 4 is not in this set.

This set of numbers includes all numbers greater than OR equal to -1. The circle on -1 is filled in to show that -1 is in this set.

Graph the sets of numbers on the number lines.

1. $x > 3$

2. $t < 1$

3. $s \geq -2$

4. $w \leq 0$

5. $y > 5 + -6$

6. $q \geq -6 - -4$

7. $r \leq 2 \cdot -2$

8. $v < \dfrac{-20}{4}$

9. $w > 15 - 17 + -1$

10. $d \leq 5 \cdot -4 + 16$

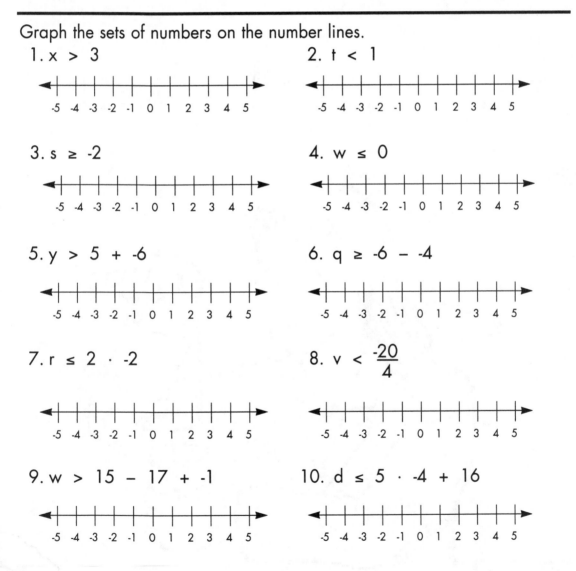

Describe the set of numbers graphed on the number lines.

11.

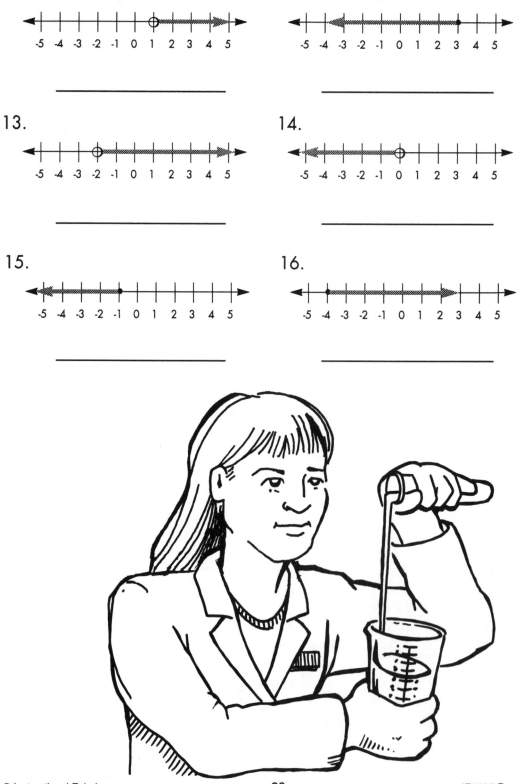

12.

_____

13.

_____

14.

_____

15.

_____

16.

_____

Mixed Review

1. $-6\frac{7}{8} + 12\frac{1}{6} =$ 2. $-8\frac{2}{3} \div -3\frac{1}{6} =$ 3. $3.14 - 6.9 =$

4. $5.4\overline{)6.75}$ 5. $\begin{array}{r} -8.03 \\ \times\ 3.7 \\ \hline \end{array}$ 6. 53% of $137.54 =

7. $6 + -2|3 + -12| =$ 8. $6.75 + 84 \div 2^2 - 15 =$

9. $16\frac{2}{3} + 18 \div 3\frac{1}{3} - 10 =$ 10. $4.75(15 - 3^3) + 2 \cdot -16 =$

11. Jones and Co. stock fell from 84⅜ to 62¼. How many points did the stock fall?

_____

12. America's Best is having a 35% off sale on their jeans. The jeans are regularly priced at $35.95. What is the sale price?

_____

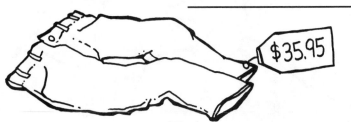

Number Statements

Mathematics is like another language. The language of mathematics is symbols. Match the symbols that represent each of the following words. Some symbols will be used more than once.

_____ 1. difference

_____ 2. product

_____ 3. percent

_____ 4. sum

_____ 5. quotient

_____ 6. more than

_____ 7. less than

_____ 8. is the same as

_____ 9. increase

_____ 10. decrease

a. +

b. –

c. x

d. ÷

e. %

f. =

5! 3-17-4?

Hello! How are you?

¡Hola! ¿Cómo estás?

Algebraic Expressions

Word Phrase	Algebraic Expression
5 more than a number	$x + 5$
the product of a number and 7	$7x$
a number divided by the sum of 6 and 3	$\dfrac{x}{6 + 3}$
3 times a number decreased by 17	$3x - 17$

Match each word phrase with its equivalent algebraic expression.

_____ 1. the sum of a number and 8

_____ 2. the product of a number and 12

_____ 3. 6 less than a number

_____ 4. -7 times a number decreased by 42

_____ 5. the quotient of a number and the absolute value of -10

_____ 6. the difference between a number and -12

_____ 7. the absolute value of the sum of 4 times a number and -8

_____ 8. a number increased by 7 then divided by 11

_____ 9. the difference between 42 and -7 times a number

_____ 10. the product of -7 and the sum of a number and 42

a. $-7x - 42$

b. $x - -12$

c. $x + 8$

d. $42 - -7x$

e. $12x$

f. $\dfrac{x + 7}{11}$

g. $x - 6$

h. $-7(x + 42)$

i. $\dfrac{x}{|-10|}$

j. $|4x + -8|$

Writing Algebraic Expressions

Write an algebraic expression for each word phrase.

1. the sum of 6 and a number   _____

2. seven more than a number   _____

3. the difference between a
    number and 17   _____

4. the product of a number and 12   _____

5. the sum of ¼ of a number and 5   _____

6. twice the difference of a number
    and 10   _____

7. five times a number divided by
    4 times a number   _____

8. a number decreased by twice
    the number   _____

9. the product of a number and 7
    increased by 11   _____

10. the quotient of 6 times a number
    and -14   _____

Solving Equations—Part 1

Variables are used in equations to represent unknown quantities. Equations are solved to determine the value of the unknown quantity. Equations are like balance scales. To keep the two sides equal, you have to do the same to both sides. If you take some away from one side without taking the same amount from the other side, the quantities would no longer be equal.

$$s + 36 = 127$$
$$s + 36 - 36 = 127 - 36$$
$$s = 91$$

Solve the equations to find the value of each variable.

1. $\quad x + 17 = 41$

   $x + 17 - \underline{\quad} = 41 - \underline{\quad}$

   $x = \underline{\quad}$

2. $\quad t - 42 = 28$

   $t - 42 + \underline{\quad} = 28 + \underline{\quad}$

   $t = \underline{\quad}$

3. $\quad 83 + y = 91$

   $83 \underline{\quad} + y = 91 \underline{\quad}$

   $y = \underline{\quad}$

4. $\quad -65 + r = 67$

   $-65 \underline{\quad} + r = 67 \underline{\quad}$

   $r = \underline{\quad}$

5. $\quad 57 + p = 26$

   $p = \underline{\quad}$

6. $\quad f - -52 = -12$

   $f = \underline{\quad}$

7. $\quad -15 + g = -41$

   $g = \underline{\quad}$

8. $\quad z + -81 = -26$

   $z = \underline{\quad}$

9. $\quad 5.7 + d = 89.6$

   $d = \underline{\quad}$

10. $\quad c - 8.97 = -52.1$

    $c = \underline{\quad}$

Solving Equations—Part 2

$$3x = 52 \qquad\qquad \frac{y}{4} = 1.7$$

$$\frac{3x}{3} = \frac{52}{3} \qquad\qquad 4 \times \frac{y}{4} = 1.7 \times 4$$

$$x = 17\frac{1}{3} \qquad\qquad y = 6.8$$

Solve these equations to find the value of the variables.

1. $4t = 112$

$$\underline{4t} = \underline{112}$$

$t = $ ___

2. $\frac{s}{6} = 15$

___ $\times \frac{s}{6} = 15 \times$ ___

$s = $ ___

3. $7w = 413$

___ $=$ ___

$w = $ ___

4. $\frac{2k}{5} = 22$

___ $\frac{2k}{5} = 22$ ___

$k = $ ___

5. $6.1a = 14.03$

$a = $ ___

6. $\frac{m}{5} = 91.3$

$m = $ ___

7. $\frac{2}{3}w = \frac{4}{7}$

$w = $ ___

8. $\frac{2w}{3} = \frac{4}{7}$

$w = $ ___

Mixed Practice Solving Equations

Find the value of the variables in these equations:

1. $3x = -21$

2. $3 + d = -19$

3. $f - -21 = 59$

4. $\frac{w}{8} = -12$

5. $\frac{-2}{3}a = -14$

6. $\frac{-2a}{3} = -14$

7. $g - 54 = 117$

8. $b + -19 = -27$

9. $5.6 + t = -1.9$

10. $-15k = -45$

11. $\frac{w}{17} = -7$

12. $3.5t = 700$

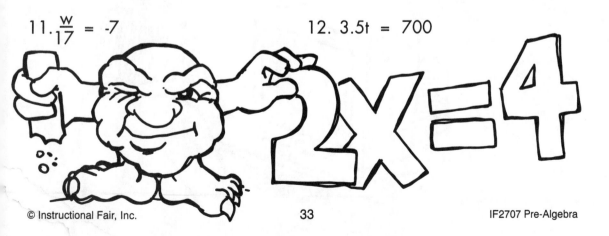

IF2707 Pre-Algebra

Problem Solving with Equations

Use equations to solve each of the problems below.

1. George was born in 1984. How old will he be in the year 2001?

   $1984 + G = 2001$

   George will be ____ years old.

2. Maria has spent $36 on school clothes. She has $24 left. How much money did Maria have before she bought the clothes?

   $m - \$36 = \$24$

   Maria had $____.

3. One computer system costs $2,100. If you add a CD Rom and modem, the cost is $2,800. How much additional is charged for the CD Rom and modem?

   Equation: _____

   Solution: _____

4. Manuel made a 31-minute long-distance phone call. He was charged $5.89. How much was Manuel charged per minute?

   Equation: _____

   Solution: _____

Solving Multi-Step Equations

Combining what you have learned on the previous pages, you can solve more involved equations.

$$3x + -18 = 24$$
$$3x + -18 - -18 = 24 - -18$$
$$\frac{3x}{3x} = \frac{42}{42}$$
$$x = 14$$

To check, replace the variable with the number you found as the solution.

$$3(14) + -18 = 24$$
$$42 + -18 = 24$$
$$24 = 24 \ \checkmark$$

---

1. $$\frac{x}{7} - 42 = -93$$

$$\frac{x}{7} - 42 \ \rule{1cm}{0.4pt} = -93 \ \rule{1cm}{0.4pt}$$

$$\frac{x}{7} = \rule{1cm}{0.4pt}$$

$$\rule{1cm}{0.4pt} \cdot \frac{x}{7} = \rule{1cm}{0.4pt} \cdot \rule{1cm}{0.4pt}$$

$$x = \rule{1cm}{0.4pt}$$

2. $-5x - 32 = -24$

3. $\frac{-2y}{7} + -15 = 16 - 42$

$$x = \rule{1cm}{0.4pt}$$

$$y = \rule{1cm}{0.4pt}$$

4. $(14 - 25)y = 27 - 4^4$

5. $\dfrac{-3t}{10} - 125 = -67$

$y =$ _____

$t =$ _____

6. $\dfrac{1}{4}f + 11 = 15 - 60$

7. $|\,18 - 21\,|x = 15 + -23$

$f =$ _____

$x =$ _____

8. $4v + 16 = 21 - 12$

9. $\dfrac{-5d}{8} - 8 = -14$

$v =$ _____

$d =$ _____

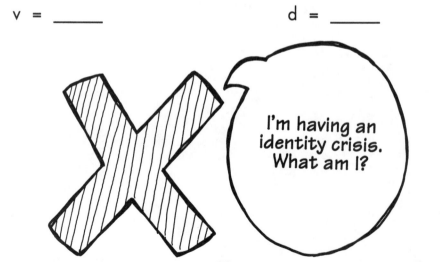

I'm having an identity crisis. What am I?

Solving Equations
(with variables on both sides)

When there are variables on both sides of the equal sign, get them together all on one side and put all the numbers on the other side.

$$2x + 17 = -6x - 12$$
$$2x - -6x + 17 = -6x - -6x - 12$$
$$8x + 17 = -12$$
$$8x + 17 - 17 = -12 - 17$$
$$8x = -29$$
$$\frac{8x}{8} = \frac{-29}{8}$$
$$x = -3\frac{5}{8}$$

---

1. $25y + 7 = 5y - 65$

2. $3v - 6\frac{3}{8} = -3v + 1\frac{1}{8}$

y = _____

v = _____

3. $5n + -17.5 = 14.6 - 5.7n$

4. $6 - c = 7c - 6$

n = _____

c = _____

IF2707 Pre-Algebra

Mixed Review

1. $-3.5 + 3^3 - |15 - 51| - 3\frac{3}{4} =$

Find the value of w if $x = 7$, $y = 2$, and $z = 0.5$

2. $w = 3x - xyz + y^x$

3. $w = x(7 - y) + yz$

Simplify each expression.

4. $41x + 32x - 12$

5. $14m + 24 - 12n - 36$

6. $3(c + d) + -7d$

7. $-3w - 7(-2y + 3w) + -3y$

Solve.

8. $8\frac{2}{3} \div -4\frac{3}{4} =$

9. 253% of $18.95 =

10. $3x - 11 = 12$

11. $\frac{2}{5}a + -6 = -17$

Problem Solving

Write an equation for each problem and solve.

1. Sara is 5 inches taller than Don. Find Don's height if Sara is 60 inches tall.

Equation: _____

Solution: _____

2. The cost of 7 binders is $27.93. Find the cost of one binder.

Equation: _____

Solution: _____

3. Bob is 67 inches tall. Bob is 15 inches less than twice Maria's height. How tall is Maria?

Equation: _____

Solution: _____

4. During the winter months, Nickie's gas bill is 3 times more than her electric and water bills combined. If Nickie's electric bill is usually $15.20 and her water bill is $11.25, how much is her winter gas bill?

Equation: _____

Solution: _____

5. The drama club sold 375 tickets for the school play. There were 4 times as many student tickets sold as adult tickets. How many adult tickets were sold?

Equation: _____

Solution: _____

6. Noel is 6 years older than David. Three times David's age decreased by 24 is Noel's age. How old are Noel and David?

Equation: _____

Solution: _____

7. Hillary has 8 times as many key chains in her collection as Yolanda has candles in her collection. If their collections total 126, how many items does each girl have in her collection?

Equation: _____

Solution: _____

8. Bernice is building a birdhouse. One board is ¾ the length of another. Eight times the sum of the length of the short board and -20 is equal to the length of the longer board decreased by 25 inches. What is the length of the longer board?

Equation: _____

Solution: _____

Solving Inequalities

Inequalities are equations that use the greater than or less than signs rather than the equal sign. Quantities on either side are not necessarily equal. Inequalities are solved in the same way as equations. There is only one minor difference. When dividing both sides of an inequality by the same number, the sign flips. Greater than becomes less than, and less than becomes greater than.

$$-9x + 27 < -6(x - 11)$$
$$-9x + 27 < -6x + 66$$
$$-9x + 6x + 27 < -6x + 6x + 66$$
$$-3x + 27 < 66$$
$$-3x + 27 - 27 < 66 - 27$$
$$-3x < 39$$
$$\frac{-3x}{-3} > \frac{39}{-3}$$

Solution set: $\qquad x > -13$

Check your answer by substituting a number from the solution set back into the original inequality. In this case, any x greater than -13 should produce a true statement. Any number equal to or less than -13 should produce a false statement.

$$x = 0$$
$$-9x + 27 < -6(x - 11)$$
$$-9(0) + 27 < -6(0 - 11)$$
$$0 + 27 < -6(-11)$$
$$27 < 66$$
true

$$x = -13$$
$$-9x + 27 < -6(x - 11)$$
$$-9(-13) + 27 < -6(-13 - 11)$$
$$117 + 27 < -6(-24)$$
$$144 < 144$$
false

Solve each inequality. Choose two numbers to check your solution. Only one should be from the solution set.

1. $\qquad 15 - g \geq 27$

Check 1: $\qquad\qquad$ Check 2:

2. $3t + \dfrac{1}{4} > -3\dfrac{2}{3}$

Check 1:   Check 2:

3. $16z + 62 \le -8(4 - 3z)$

Check 1:   Check 2:

Mixed Practice

Simplify.

1. $3x + 2y - 32(x - y)$

2. $-4(14e - 3c) + 21e$

Solve.

3. $3x - 12 = 62$

4. $\dfrac{3m}{4} = |\ 16 - 24\ |$

5. $7(x - 4) = 16 + 32x$

6. $19 - 7x + 13 + 24x = -19$

Find the solution set and graph on the number line.

7. $\dfrac{-6x}{7} + 49 \geq 52$

8. $8(4 - x) < 57 - 61$

Plotting Points

Ordered pairs are the directions needed to get from the **origin**, the center of a coordinate graph, to a specific point. The first number tells you how far to move left or right. This is the same as finding a point on a number line. The second number tells you how far to move up or down.

The point (5, -6) tells you to start at the origin and move 5 spaces to the right and 6 spaces down.

Plot the following points. Connect them in order.

(3, 2)
(7, 0)
(2, -1)
(2, -6)
(-1, -1)
(-7, -2)
(-3, 2)
(-6, 7)
(-1, 4)
(4, 8)
(3, 2)

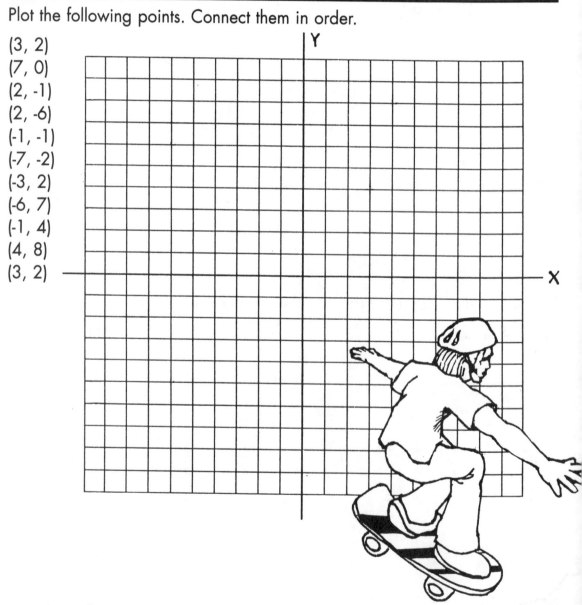

Use the grid below to create your own dot-to-dot picture. Write down the coordinate points and give them to a friend to see if he or she can plot them correctly.

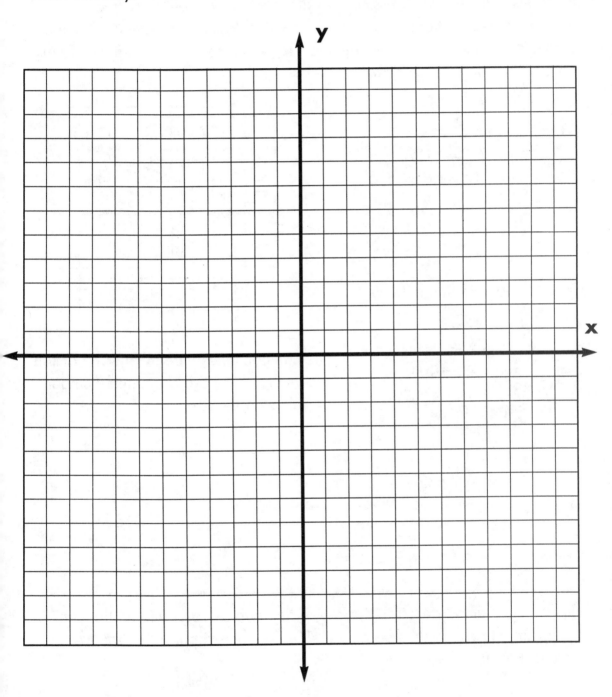

Graphing Equations

Equations with two variables can be graphed on a coordinate grid. Graphic representations of equations are used to solve problems. One way to graph any line is to choose numbers to substitute for one variable. Then solve to find the other variable.

$$x - 3y = -10$$

What if x were 5?

$$5 - 3y = -10$$
$$5 - 5 - 3y = -10 - 5$$
$$-3y = -15$$
$$\frac{-3y}{-3} = \frac{-15}{-3}$$
$$y = 5$$

One point on the line is (5, 5).

What if x were -1.

$$-1 - 3y = -10$$
$$-1 + 1 - 3y = -10 + 1$$
$$-3y = -9$$
$$\frac{-3y}{-3} = \frac{-9}{-3}$$
$$y = 3$$

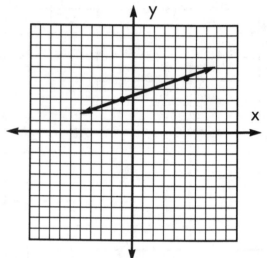

The line continues indefinitely. The graph shows that there are an infinite number of points on the line.

Another point on the line is (-1, 3).

1. Use the method described above to find two more points on the line having the equation x – 3y = -10. Use the graph of the line to check your answers.

(_____ , _____) and (_____ , _____)

Find two points, then graph each line.
  2. x + y = 10

  3. 3x − 2y = 6

  4. y = 2x − 1

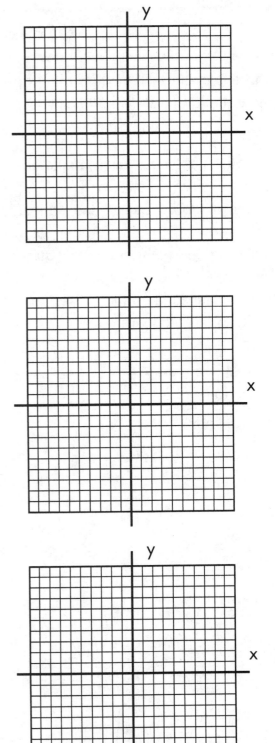

Solving for y

There is a short-cut method for graphing equations. But, in order to use it, the equation must be in this form:

$$y = mx + b$$

Equations are easily put in this form by solving for y. To solve for y, you move everything but y over to the right side of the equal sign. But you cannot just move around numbers in an equation. What you do to one side, you must do to the other to keep the values on either side balanced.

$$3x + 2y = -10$$
$$3x - 3x + 2y = -3x - 10$$
$$2y = -3x - 10$$
$$\frac{2y}{2} = \frac{-3x - 10}{2}$$
$$y = \frac{-3x}{2} - \frac{10}{2}$$
$$y = \frac{-3y}{2} - 5$$

Solve for y.

1. $x + y = 17$

2. $x - y = -10$

3. $3x = y - 11$

4. $5y = -2x + 15$

Slope

Another key to using the short cut to graphing is to understand slope. In the equation y = mx + b, m stands for slope. The slope of a hill tells how steep the hill is. The same is true for the slope of a line.

Slope is given a numerical value by finding two points and noticing the change in y and the change in x. (0, 2) and (4, 7) are two points on the line at the right.

Slope = $\dfrac{\textbf{change in y}}{\textbf{change in x}}$

Slope = $\dfrac{7 - 2}{4 - 0}$

Slope = $\dfrac{5}{4}$

Pick any two points on the same line and the slope should be the same.
Consider (-4, -3) and (4, 7)

Slope = $\dfrac{7 - \text{-}3}{4 - \text{-}4}$

Slope = $\dfrac{10}{8} = \dfrac{5}{4}$

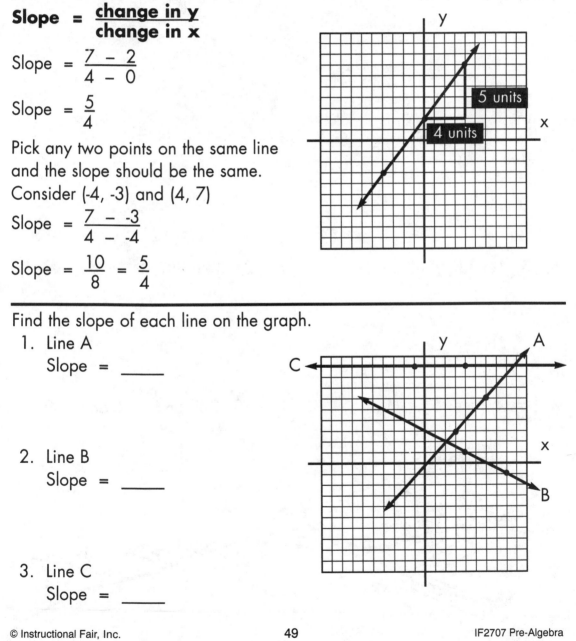

Find the slope of each line on the graph.

1. Line A
   Slope = _____

2. Line B
   Slope = _____

3. Line C
   Slope = _____

$$\text{Slope} = \frac{\text{change in y}}{\text{change in x}} = \frac{\text{difference in y-values}}{\text{difference in x-values}}$$

$$\text{Slope} = \frac{y_2 - y_1}{x_2 - x_1}$$

To find slope, subtract the two y-values and the two x-values.

Use the formula to find the slope of a line having the following pairs of points.

1. (2, 3) and (6, 9)

2. (0, 5) and (4, -7)

3. (6, -1) and (-5, 5)

4. (8, 4) and (4, 1)

5. (-5, -1) and (-2, -4)

6. (-4, -5) and (0, 0)

7. $(4\frac{1}{3}, -5)$ and $(6\frac{1}{3}, -4)$

8. (4.5, -3.2) and (-6.1 and 7.4)

Finding Equations

When a line is in the form of $y = mx + b$, you can graph it using a short-cut. You know how to get an equation into that form. You know what slope is. Now, what does the b stand for? b represents the **y-intercept,** or the place where the line crosses the y-axis. The y-intercept for the line at the right is 4. The slope of the line is ⅔. So, the equation of this line must be

$$y = -\frac{2}{3}x + 4$$

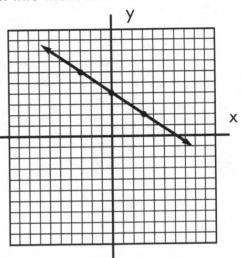

Write the equation for each line on the graph.

1. Line A

_____

2. Line B

_____

3. Line C

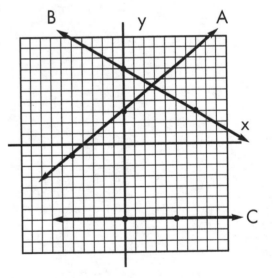

_____

Graph each of the following lines using the short-cut method. If necessary, solve for y to get the equation in the right form.

Graphing Using the Short-Cut Method

1. $y = 3x + 7$

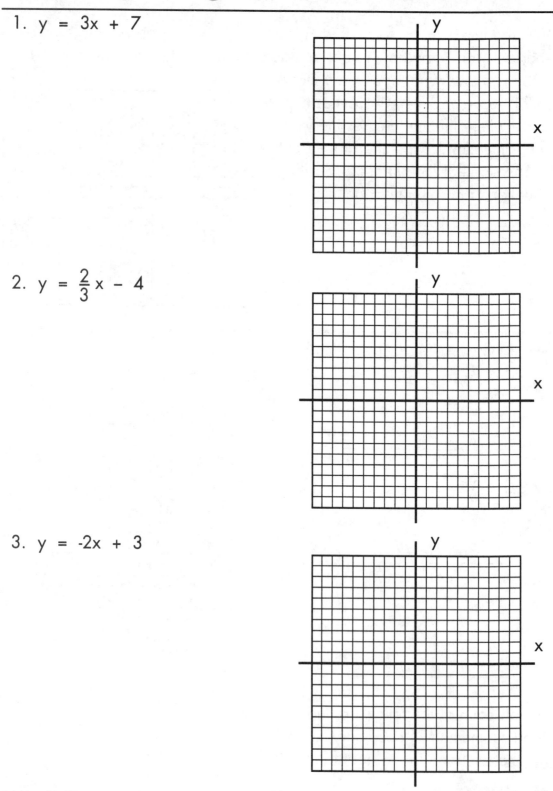

2. $y = \frac{2}{3}x - 4$

3. $y = -2x + 3$

4. $3y = -2x - 6$

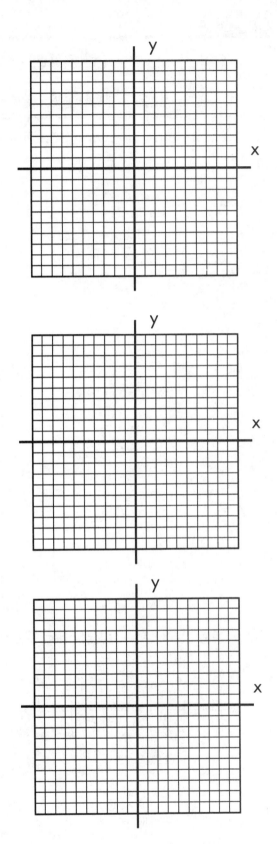

5. $2x + y = 8$

6. $-3x - 2y = 12$

 IF2707 Pre-Algebra

Mixed Review
Equations and Inequalities

Solve each of the following equations and inequalities.

1. $3x = 3.15$

2. $x - 2\frac{7}{8} = 5\frac{1}{12}$

3. $9x + 15 = 32$

4. $\frac{2x}{5} - 51 = 29$

5. $62 - x < 27$

6. $\frac{x}{2.5} \geq 13$

7. $3(5 - x) > 27$

8. $14x + 27 \leq 27x - 12$

Graph the solutions for problem 7 and 8 on the number lines.

9.

10.

Mixed Review

Solve the following problems:

1. $6\frac{3}{8} + 3\frac{7}{12} =$

2. $8\frac{1}{3} - 4\frac{5}{9} =$

3. $5.13 + 6.1 + 3.17 =$

4. $14.29 - 1.00004 =$

5. $\frac{2}{5} \times 6\frac{1}{8} \times 2\frac{1}{7} =$

6. $18\frac{1}{9} \div 3\frac{1}{4} =$

7. $6.14 \times 0.075 =$

8. $4.1\overline{)15.17}$

9. $2^8 + 3 - 15 \cdot 2 =$

10. $5(8 - 12) + 4\,|8 - 12\,| =$

11. $51 + -12 =$

12. $16 - -14 + -10 =$

13. Find the value of w if $x = 1$, $y = 6$, and $z = -3$

   $w = 4x - yz + 6^x$

14. Write the symbolic form for each word phrase.
   a. six less than twice a number

   b. a number divided by -10 and increased by 11

Simplify.

15. $3(x - 11) + 4y - 16x$

16. $4x + 3y - 2x + z$

Solve each equation.

17. $8x - 11 = -15$

18. $\dfrac{-2x}{3} - 15 = 21$

Answer Key

Fractions, Decimals, and Percents

Adding and Subtracting Fractions — page 1
1. 12
2. 9
3. 18
4. $\frac{9}{10}$
5. $1\frac{1}{28}$
6. $1\frac{3}{10}$
7. $\frac{5}{18}$
8. $\frac{9}{15}$
9. $\frac{4}{9}$
10. $\frac{7}{8}$ yd

Multiplying Fractions — page 2
1. $\frac{7}{20}$
2. $\frac{1}{6}$
3. $\frac{2}{3}$
4. $\frac{3}{8}$
5. $\frac{7}{30}$
6. $\frac{5}{9}$
7. $\frac{1}{15}$
8. $\frac{3}{11}$
9. $\frac{3}{4}$
10. $\frac{9}{55}$
11. $\frac{9}{13}$
12. $\frac{39}{5}$
13. $\frac{49}{285}$
14. $\frac{17}{40}$

Dividing Fractions — page 3
1. $24 divided by 3
2. $24 times 1/3
3. $1\frac{1}{2}$
4. $\frac{17}{21}$
5. $1\frac{1}{3}$
6. 15
7. $1\frac{5}{28}$
8. $\frac{7}{10}$
9. $\frac{8}{21}$
10. $\frac{18}{35}$
11. $\frac{224}{289}$

Working with Mixed Numbers — page 4
1. $8\frac{5}{8}$
2. $3\frac{17}{24}$
3. $20\frac{4}{15}$
4. $9\frac{5}{8}$
5. $63\frac{5}{8}$
6. $4\frac{24}{25}$
7. $26\frac{5}{8}$
8. $17\frac{1}{4}$
9. 144
10. $3\frac{5}{8}$
11. $2\frac{47}{50}$
12. $1\frac{56}{57}$

Problem Solving with Fractions — page 5
1. $56\frac{2}{3}$ yds.
2. $183\frac{1}{3}$ sq. yds.
3. 4 posts
4. $\frac{1}{3}$ yd.
5. 24 posts

Adding and Subtracting Decimals — page 6
1. 73.24
2. 41.3
3. 175.31
4. 42.93
5. 12.52
6. 75.77
7. 64.48
8. 23.44
9. 13.66
10. 1.41 mg
11. 2.22 mg

Multiplying and Dividing Decimals — page 7
1. 11.832
2. 1.857
3. 0.098
4. 73.13684
5. 1023.75
6. 0.04
7. 3.14
8. 78
9. 5.7

Percents — page 8
1. 0.4, 40%
2. 0.75, 75%
3. $\frac{1}{4}$, 25%
4. $\frac{27}{40}$, 67.5%
5. $\frac{1}{2}$, 0.5
6. $\frac{7}{8}$, 0.875
7. 6.7, 670%
8. $4\frac{4}{5}$, 480%
9. $6\frac{1}{4}$, 6.25

Working with Percents — page 9
1. 48
2. 270
3. $93.75
4. $3.91
5. 0.91
6. 256.2
7. $137.80
8. CDs $12.60/Cassettes-$9
9. yes

Problem Solving with Decimals — page 10
1. yes
2. The CD normally sells for about $25. The discount is greater than the sales tax percentage. So the total price cannot be more than $25.
3. 55%–$6.75, 30% then 25%–$7.87
4. no–$66.71

Mixed Review — page 11
1. $10\frac{23}{24}$
2. $5\frac{23}{40}$
3. 57
4. 4.7
5. 1.2222
6. 218.21
7. $7\frac{1}{3}$
8. $1\frac{5}{8}$
9. 31.885
10. 0.125, 125%
11. $1\frac{7}{10}$, 170%
12. $\frac{13}{20}$, 0.65
13. 1 test
14. $92.50

Integers and Rational Numbers

What Are Integers? — page 12
1. <
2. >
3. >
4. <
5. >
6. >
7. =
8. >
9. =
10. <
11. >
12. <
13. 6
14. 6
15. 8

Adding Integers — page 13
1. 1
2. 4
3. 8
4. -5
5. -3
6. 2
7. 11
8. -11
9. 0
10. 0
11. -8
12. 12
13. -4
14. -1
15. 2
16. -12
17. -36
18. 10
19. $-8

Subtracting Integers — page 14
1. 1
2. -4
3. -4
4. -3
5. 0
6. -2
7. 13
8. 13
9. 6
10. 3
11. -4
12. 4

Multiplying and Dividing Integers — page 15

1. -16
2. -6
3. 0
4. -42
5. -32
6. -56
7. 12
8. 36
9. 9
10. -5
11. 4
12. -8
13. -5
14. -9
15. 9
16. -312
17. -25
18. 1000
19. -144

Mixed Review — page 16

1. ¾
2. 5.1
3. 109.227
4. 10⁷⁄₂₄
5. 4⅞
6. 17.446
7. 10.29
8. 133.12
9. 5
10. 19
11. -35
12. 11
13. -105
14. 28
15. 16

Order of Operations — page 17

2. 23
3. 348
4. -62
5. -62

Rational Numbers — page 18

1. $^{-23}\!/_{24}$
2. -23¹⁷⁄₁₈
3. -1⅕
4. 1⁵¹⁄₅₃
5. 4.27
6. 67.35
7. 204.189
8. -1.37
9. down 9¼

Comparing Rational Numbers — page 19

1. <
2. <
3. >
4. <
5. <
6. >
7. >
8. >
9. <
10. >

Mixed Review — page 20

1. $^{-11}\!/_{24}$
2. 7.72
3. 56⁵⁄₂₇
4. 7
5. -31.62
6. -30
7. -39.955
8. 16
9. 15
10. 464
11. <
12. >
13. >
14. <

Variables

Letter Soup — page 21

1. y = 36
2. y = 24.3
3. x = 297.7
4. x = -7.51

page 22

5. d = 25
6. d = 182
7. w = -183
8. w = -1
9. a = -8
10. a = 10
11. t = 22
12. 5 = 1.331

Simplifying Expressions — page 23

1. 6x - 3
2. 8y - 4.15
3. 2g - f
4. 24xy + 16x -3z
5. 44 - 40st
6. 2rs - 8r
7. y - 2⅛x
8. 7a - 9
9. -10vw + 8v -6w
10. -3x - 14

Number Lines — page 24

1. G
2. B
3. E
4. A
5. H
6. D
7. F
8. I
9. C

Variables and Number Lines — page 25

1. x > 3
2. t < 1
3. s ≥ -2
4. w ≠ 0
5. y > -1
6. q ≥ -2
7. r ≤ -4
8. v < -5
9. w > -3
10. d ≤ -4

11. x > 1
12. x ≤ 3
13. x > -2
14. x < 0
15. x ≤ -1
16. x ≥ -4

Mixed Review — page 27

1. 5⁷⁄₂₄
2. 2¹⁴⁄₁₉
3. -3.76
4. 1.25
5. -29.711
6. $72.90
7. -12
8. 12.75
9. 12¹⁄₁₅
10. -89
11. 22⅛
12. $23.37

Number Statements — page 28

1. b
2. c
3. e
4. a
5. d
6. a
7. b
8. f
9. a
10. b

Algebraic Expressions — page 29

1. c
2. e
3. g
4. a
5. i
6. b
7. j
8. f
9. d
10. h

Writing Algebraic Expressions — page 30

1. 6 + x
2. x + 7
3. x - 17
4. 12x
5. ¼x + 5
6. 2(x - 10)
7. $^{5x}\!/_{4x}$
8. x - 2x
9. 7x + 11
10. $^{6x}\!/_{-14}$

Equations and Inequalities

Solving Equations—Part 1 — page 31
1. 17, 17, 24
2. 42, 42, 70
3. -83, -83, 8
4. +65, +65, 132
5. -31
6. -64
7. -26
8. 55
9. 83.9
10. -43.13

Solving Equations—Part 2 — page 32
1. 4, 4, 28
2. 6, 6, 90
3. $^{7w}/_7$, $^{413}/_7$, 59
4. $^5/_2 x$, $x^5/_2$, 55
5. 2.3
6. 456.5
7. $^6/_7$
8. $^6/_7$

Mixed Practice Solving Equations — page 33
1. x = -7
2. d = -22
3. f = 38
4. w = -96
5. a = 21
6. a = 21
7. g = 171
8. b = -8
9. 5 = -7.5
10. k = 3
11. w = -119
12. 5 = 200

Problem Solving with Equations — page 34
1. 17
2. $60
3. $2,100 + x = $2,800
   x = $700
4. 31x = $5.89
   x = $0.19

Solving Multi-Step Equations — page 35
1. +42, +42
   -51
   7, -51, 7
   -357
2. $^{-6}/_5$ or $-1^1/_5$
3. $38^1/_2$
4. $20^9/_{11}$
5. $-193^1/_3$
6. -224
7. $^{-8}/_3$ or $-2^2/_3$
8. $^{-7}/_4$ or $-1^3/_4$
9. $9^3/_5$

Solving Equations — page 37
1. $-3^3/_5$
2. $1^1/_4$
3. 3
4. $^3/_2$ or $1^1/_2$

Mixed Review — page 38
1. -16.25
2. w = 142
3. w = 36
4. 73x - 12
5. 14m - 12n - 12
6. 3c - 4d
7. -24w + 11y
8. $-1^{47}/_{57}$
9. $47.94
10. $x = 7^2/_3$
11. $a = -27^1/_2$

Problem Solving — page 39
1. d + 5 = 60
   d = 55
   Don's height is 55 inches

2. 7b = $27.93
   b = $3.99
   Each binder costs $3.99
3. 2m - 15 = 67
   m = 41
   Maria is 41 inches tall
4. g = 3 ($15.20 + $11.25)
   g = $79.35
   Nickie's winter gas bill is $79.35

page 40
5. 4a + a = 375
   a = 75
   There were 75 adult tickets sold.
6. 3d - 24 = d + 6
   d = 15
   David is 15. Noel is 21.
7. 8c + c = 126
   9c = 126
   c = 14
   Yolanda has 14 candles.
   Hillary has 112 key chains.
8. 8($^3/_4 x$ + -20) = x - 25
   x = 27
   The longer board measures 27 inches.

Solving Inequalities — page 41
1. g ≤ -12
   Check 1: Answers will vary.
   Check 2: Answers will vary.
2. t > $-1^{11}/_{36}$
   Check 1: Answers will vary.
   Check 2: Answers will vary.
3. z ≥ $11^3/_4$
   Check 1: Answers will vary.
   Check 2: Answers will vary.

Mixed Practice — page 43
1. -29x + 34y
2. -35e + 12c
3. $x = 24^2/_3$
4. $m = 10^2/_3$
5. $x = -1^{19}/_{25}$
6. x = -3
7. $x ≤ -3^1/_2$
8. $x > 4^1/_2$

Graphing

Plotting Points — page 44

Graphing Equations — page 46

1. Answers will vary. Two possible points are (-10, 0) and (-7, 1)

Graphing Equations — page 47

2.. 3., and 4. Points will vary.

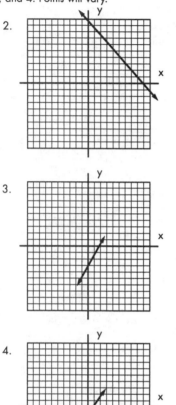

2.

3.

4.

Solving for y — page 48

1. $y = 17 - x$
2. $y = x + 10$
3. $3x + 11 = y$
4. $y = \frac{2}{3}x + 3$

Slope — page 49

1. 1
2. $-\frac{1}{2}$
3. 0

1. ¾ or ½
2. -3
3. $\frac{5}{11}$
4. ¾
5. -1
6. ¾
7. ½
8. -1

Finding Equations — page 51

1. $y = \frac{4}{5}x + 3$
2. $y = -\frac{4}{7} + 7$
3. $y = -7$

Graphing Using the Short-Cut Method — pages 52 and 53

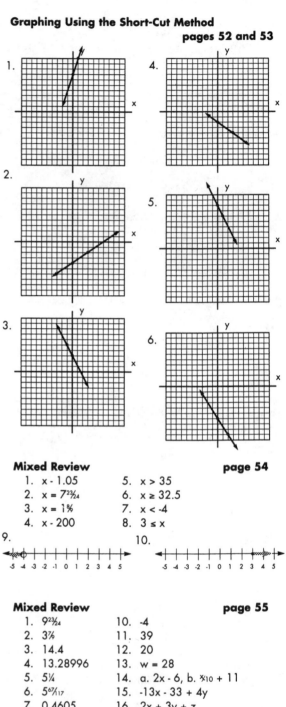

1.

2.

3.

4.

5.

6.

Mixed Review — page 54

1. x - 1.05
2. $x = 7^{23}\!/_{24}$
3. $x = 1\frac{5}{6}$
4. x - 200
5. x > 35
6. x ≥ 32.5
7. x < -4
8. 3 ≤ x

9. [number line from -5 to 5]

10. [number line from -5 to 5]

Mixed Review — page 55

1. $9^{23}\!/_{24}$
2. 3⅞
3. 14.4
4. 13.28996
5. 5¼
6. $5^{6}\!/_{17}$
7. 0.4605
8. 3.7
9. 229
10. -4
11. 39
12. 20
13. w = 28
14. a. 2x - 6, b. $\frac{x}{10}$ + 11
15. -13x - 33 + 4y
16. 2x + 3y + z
17. $x = -\frac{1}{2}$
18. x = -54